WILLIAM HOWARD Taft

WILLIAM HOWARD *Taft*

OUR TWENTY-SEVENTH PRESIDENT

By Melissa Maupin

SPIRIT
of America™

The Child's World®, Inc.
Chanhassen, Minnesota

WILLIAM HOWARD *Taft*

Published in the United States of America by The Child's World®, Inc.
PO Box 326 • Chanhassen, MN 55317-0326 • 800-599-READ • www.childsworld.com

Acknowledgments
The Creative Spark: Mary Francis-DeMarois, Project Director; Elizabeth Sirimarco Budd, Series Editor; Robert Court, Design and Art Direction; Janine Graham, Page Layout; Jennifer Moyers, Production

The Child's World®, Inc.: Mary Berendes, Publishing Director; Red Line Editorial, Fact Research; Cindy Klingel, Curriculum Advisor; Robert Noyed, Historical Advisor

Photos
Cover: White House Collection, courtesy White House Historical Association; The Library of Congress: 6, 11, 12, 14, 19, 20-21, 22, 23, 26, 26, 27, 28, 29, 30, 31, 32, 33; William Howard Taft National Historic Site: 7, 8, 9, 10, 13, 17

Registration
The Child's World®, Inc., Spirit of America™, and their associated logos are the sole property and registered trademarks of The Child's World®, Inc.

Library of Congress Cataloging-in-Publication Data
Maupin, Melissa, 1958–
    William Howard Taft : our 27th president / by Melissa Maupin.
        p. cm.
        Includes bibliographical references and index.
    ISBN 1-56766-835-6 (lib. bdg. : alk. paper)
    1. Taft, William H. (William Howard), 1857–1930—Juvenile literature. 2. Presidents—United States—Biography—Juvenile literature. [1. Taft, William H. (William Howard), 1857–1930.
2. Presidents.] I. Title.
    E762 .M18 2001
    973.91'2'092—dc21
                                                                00-010575

10   19   29

Contents

Chapter ONE

A Legacy of Law

William Howard Taft was the nation's 27th president, but the work he truly loved was the law. Taft is the only person to have served as both the president and as the chief justice of the Supreme Court.

YOUNG WILLIAM HOWARD TAFT DREAMED OF becoming a judge, just as his father, Alphonso, had been. Alphonso Taft was not only a well-respected judge, he also served as the **secretary of war** under President Ulysses S. Grant. As a child, the younger Taft heard stories about his father's work and travel. He longed to follow in his successful father's footsteps. By the end of his career, he would reach his goal and achieve success even beyond that of his father. One day, William Taft would become the only man in history to have the honor of serving both as the president of the United States and as **chief justice** of the **Supreme Court.**

William Taft was born in Cincinnati, Ohio, on September 15, 1857. He was a healthy, happy child who laughed easily. Taft's mother,

Louise, and his father believed strongly in education. They pushed William to study and make good grades. He was a bright and eager student.

Taft attended Yale University in Connecticut, just as his father and older half-brothers had. Yale was among the very best colleges in the country. Taft was popular with the other students, who enjoyed his good nature and sense of humor. They nicknamed him "Big Bill" because by then, Taft stood six feet, two inches tall and was stocky in build.

In 1878, he graduated second in his class at Yale and enrolled at Cincinnati Law School. Taft graduated from law school in 1880 and became licensed to practice law. Instead of working at a law firm, Taft landed his first job working as a court reporter for a Cincinnati newspaper, the *Commercial Gazette*.

Taft, shown here with his mother, grew up in a respected, well-to-do Ohio family.

Alphonso Taft (above) was a successful man, and William followed in his father's footsteps. Like his father, William became a lawyer, a judge, and then the secretary of war. But William surpassed even his father's achievements when he became the 27th U.S. president.

Taft's job as reporter was the last one for which he ever **applied.** From that time forward, he was **appointed** to a variety of jobs in the government. People liked his skill, intellect, and friendly style. Taft accepted his first appointment just one year out of law school. He left his job as court reporter to work as the assistant **prosecutor** of Hamilton County. Then, in 1882, President Chester Arthur appointed him the tax collector for the Cincinnati area. He was the youngest tax collector in the country at that time.

At age 29, Taft filled a vacancy on the Ohio State Superior Court. He was thrilled with this opportunity because more than anything, Taft wanted to be a judge. At this point in his career, he already had begun to dream of sitting on the bench of the highest (most powerful) court in the country, the United States Supreme Court.

During his early career, Taft fell in love with his future wife, Helen Herron, whom he called Nellie. Taft visited Nellie at her home, where young adults gathered and talked about popular books they had read. Like Taft's mother, Nellie was an intelligent, well-educated woman from a respected family. By this time, Taft weighed 240 pounds. It was the beginning of his lifelong struggle with weight gain.

William Taft (in the center of the doorway) is shown here in 1878 with his classmates at Yale University. Taft graduated as the second-best student in his class. His parents were somewhat disappointed that he was not the valedictorian, the very best student of all.

Interesting Facts

▶ When "little Willie" Taft was seven years old, his mother wrote that he was "very large for his age" and grew fatter every day. She said he had such a large waist that he couldn't wear baby clothes with belts.

▶ Taft suffered a serious accident when he was nine years old. He was riding in a horse-drawn carriage when the horse was startled and ran away. The carriage was wrecked, and Taft was dragged along, his head bumping on the ground. He nearly died from the accident and had to have many stitches on his skull, leaving him with a large scar.

Nellie was cool to Taft at first, and he worried that she would never marry him. Finally, she made him a happy man by accepting his proposal of marriage. They wed on June 19, 1886, and later had three children: Charles, Helen, and Robert. The Tafts' marriage was the beginning of a strong partnership. Nellie's opinions and her faith in her husband's abilities would play an important role in his future.

On a winter evening in 1879, Taft met Nellie Herron at a sledding party. He soon joined a club that Nellie had started to discuss books and other intellectual topics. Taft (center) and Nellie (seated at his right), shown here with other members of the club, soon fell in love and married.

10

WILLIAM TAFT IS THE most famous member of his family, but Cincinnati's Taft family has a long tradition of education and success. Taft's great grandfather, Aaron Taft, graduated from Princeton University and worked as a town clerk. His grandfather, Peter, was a judge, justice of the peace, and a member of the Vermont State Legislature, the group of people elected to make laws for that state. Taft's father, Alphonso, felt strongly that any government appointment was an honor. Alphonso was a judge and served as the secretary of war, just as his son would one day.

Taft's two older half-brothers, Charles and Peter, both graduated from Yale and practiced law. Charles later became a U.S. congressman. Taft's younger brothers, Harry and Horace, both graduated from Yale, too. Harry went on to practice law, and Horace opened a school for boys.

The tradition continued with the next generations. Both of William Taft's sons became lawyers. The oldest, Robert, was a leading U.S. senator. His younger son, Charles, was elected the mayor of Cincinnati. Taft's grandson, Robert Jr., also became a U.S. senator. His great grandson, Robert III, was elected governor of Ohio in 1999.

Chapter TWO

Climbing the Political Ladder

Taft might never have become the president without his wife's encouragement and ambition. In a letter to his beloved Nellie, Taft once wrote, "Oh, how I will work and strive to be better and do better, how I will labor for our joint advancement if you will only let me."

AT AGE 32, WILLIAM TAFT LEARNED THAT President Benjamin Harrison was thinking of appointing him to the Supreme Court. He felt honored but knew he probably would not get the position. He was simply too young and inexperienced for such an important appointment. Taft joked that his chances of winning the position were about equal to his chances of "going to the moon." Instead, Harrison offered him the position of **solicitor** general. The solicitor general helps the most important lawyer in the country, the attorney general. Mrs. Taft felt this offer was a great opportunity for her husband, and she liked the idea of moving to the nation's capital city. She and Taft's family encouraged him to take the job.

Two years later, 34-year-old Taft heard that a place was opening on the United States **Circuit Court.** This was one of the highest courts in the country, second only to the Supreme Court. Taft truly wanted the position, and to his delight, it was offered to him. He moved his family from Washington back to Cincinnati and began traveling to several cities to hear trials. Nellie was not as pleased with the change as her husband was. She felt that

Taft should stay in Washington, D.C., where he could meet the most powerful people in **politics.** Taft did not care for political life, however. He felt more comfortable in the courtroom dealing with the law.

Taft served on the circuit court from 1892 until 1900. In this position, he **ruled** on many issues involving the workplace. At this time in the United States, many workers were not paid fairly for their work. Others worked in crowded, unhealthy, and dangerous places. Children also commonly worked in factories. Many of them did not go to school. They worked long hours and performed dangerous jobs, just like the adults in the factory.

Unhappy workers began to band together to form **labor unions.** The unions demanded fair working conditions and pay. Some unions went on **strike.** They refused to work until they got what they wanted. Business owners grew angry and refused to give in to the employees. Some unions then used violence when they did not get their way.

As a judge, Taft made enemies with some leaders of the labor unions. He believed the workers deserved better treatment, but he also

14

believed that the labor unions should obey the law. When the labor unions broke the law or used violence to get their way, they often went to court. If Taft felt they had broken the law, he ruled against them.

One day in 1900, Taft received a message from President McKinley offering him a surprising challenge. The United States had just finished fighting the Spanish-American War. In the **treaty** that ended the war, Spain gave the United States control of the Philippine Islands, located in the Pacific Ocean southeast of Asia. President McKinley was sending a **commission** to take control of the islands. He asked Taft to serve as the commission president.

Taft did not feel qualified for this position. Again, Nellie and his family encouraged him to accept the job. The U.S. secretary of war, Elihu Root, also urged him to take the job. Finally, Taft decided to try his hand at governing the islands.

When Taft reached the Philippines, he realized what a difficult job lay ahead of him. The country was made up of more than 7,000 islands, and the people spoke seven different languages. Most of the people lived in poor conditions. There were no schools, and the

Although life in the Philippines was difficult, Taft did his best to help the people. "Always in my heart the Philippines have had the first place," Taft once said. "I love the noble Filipino people."

government was unstable. Outbreaks of violence among the people were also common.

Taft traveled on horseback throughout the Philippines, getting to know the people. Soon they grew to trust him. In 1901, Taft became the official governor of the islands. He enjoyed working with the Filipino people. He created a plan to help them set up their own government. His first steps were to construct a good road system and to organize local governments. Next, he worked to set up schools, courts, and basic services for the people.

Unfortunately, life in the Philippines was uncomfortable at times. The climate was hot and steamy. There were mosquitoes and violent tropical storms. Taft suffered from severe stomach problems and other difficulties that made him ill. Even with these health problems, he weighed close to 300 pounds. The extra weight made the trips across the islands on horseback even more uncomfortable. Taft still took his position in the Philippines seriously and did the best job he could.

16

WHEN TAFT LEFT FOR THE PHILIPPINES IN 1900, HE TOOK HIS FAMILY WITH him. This photograph shows William Taft at left with Filipino children and other members of the commission to the islands. Nellie is standing third from right. Their son Robert (center) was 10 years old when they left for the Philippines. (Two other children—daughter Helen, age eight, and little Charlie, age two—are not shown.)

Mrs. Taft was especially excited about the chance to travel so far from home. She read everything she could find about the Philippines. The family sailed to Hawaii and then Japan. Finally, they arrived in the Philippine city of Manila, where they would live for the next four years.

The time spent in the Philippines was mostly happy for the Tafts. They had a Chinese cook and several servants, but their day-to-day life was simple. Mrs. Taft traveled with her husband all around the islands. The children made friends and attended school. They rode ponies and kept a monkey, an orangutan, and a deer as pets. They even learned to speak the local language.

Chapter THREE

Pressured into the Presidency

The nation was shocked and saddened to learn that President McKinley (above) was assassinated on September 6, 1901. He was the third U.S. president to be murdered and the last to walk among the people without protection from the secret service.

SEPTEMBER 1901 WAS A TIME OF SORROW FOR America. Taft was in the Philippines when word reached him that President McKinley had been **assassinated.** The news stunned and saddened him. He respected President McKinley, who had supported his efforts in the Philippines.

Vice President Theodore Roosevelt took McKinley's place for the rest of the term. Taft was unsure of Roosevelt's opinion about the Philippines. He was relieved to learn that Roosevelt admired his work.

When a position opened on the Supreme Court, Roosevelt offered Taft the seat. Taft turned the offer down, even though he longed to accept it. He felt that he should finish his work in the Philippines first.

Theodore Roosevelt (left) became president after McKinley's death. He respected Taft (right) and eventually asked him to join his cabinet. The two men became close friends and coworkers. Taft once wrote of Roosevelt, "The president seems really to take much comfort that I am in his cabinet."

When Roosevelt was elected for his second term as president, he asked Taft to become a member of his **cabinet** as the secretary of war. This opportunity came at a good time for Taft. His work in the Philippines was nearly finished. He had also grown very ill. He needed to return to the United States to recover.

One of the most important things that Taft did during his time as the secretary of war was to oversee the building of the Panama Canal. He made sure the job was done well with few problems along the way.

Because of his sense of fairness and his likable personality, Taft proved to be an excellent secretary of war. He managed to calm leaders and rebels in Cuba following a **revolution.** He also helped write a treaty between Japan and Russia following the Russo-Japanese War. Then Roosevelt sent him to Panama to oversee the building of the Panama Canal. This 50-mile-long canal would cut through the land and allow ships to cross from the Atlantic to the Pacific Ocean. Ships no longer had to travel all the way around the tip of South America to get from one ocean to the other.

Roosevelt's presidency was about to end. Many members of the Republican **political party** thought Taft should run for president. At age 51, he had decades of experience in many different government jobs. Yet Taft shied

away from the presidency. He still pictured himself as a judge, not as the **chief executive.** Taft wanted Roosevelt or Elihu Root to run, but neither man would. They both urged Taft to run for the Republican Party **nomination.**

Nellie had longed for many years to see her husband become president. She and his brothers pushed him to run for the nomination. Only Taft's mother recognized the true nature of her son. "I do not want my son to be president," she said. "His is a judicial mind and he loves the law."

It looked as if a man named William Jennings Bryan, who ran for president in several elections, would likely be the Democratic Party's **candidate.** When Taft learned this, he made the decision to run. He thought Bryan's ideas about how to run the government

21

were **radical.** He believed that if Bryan were president, he might ruin the country.

Taft leaned heavily on Roosevelt for support as he ran for office. Nellie grew irritated because he constantly mentioned Roosevelt's name in his **campaign** speeches. She wanted her husband to appear confident and independent. But Taft felt more confident having Roosevelt's support.

Taft and the vice presidential candidate, James Sherman, won the election of 1908. A terrible blizzard blew in on the day of their **inauguration.** Taft joked, "I always said it would be a cold day when I got to be president of the United States." The bad weather may have been a sign of how miserable his presidency would be.

One of Taft's first problems as president was that people wanted him to be like Theodore Roosevelt. Roosevelt and Taft were very different. Roosevelt was good at selling his ideas to Congress and to the public. Taft was a quieter, more private man. As president, he tended to avoid arguments and did not push his ideas.

President Taft began his term trying to continue Roosevelt's **progressive** work. The progressive Republicans wanted to improve life for the average citizen. They worked to pass laws that would help small businesses and farmers.

On the other hand, the **conservative** Republicans in Congress were loyal to big businesses. They believed that government should not interfere with business. Two powerful senators, Nelson Aldrich and Joseph Cannon, stopped many **bills** that the progressives tried to pass.

Taft had difficulty working with the conservative Republicans. Unlike Roosevelt, he believed that the president had limited power. He did not think a president should use his power to make Congress pass certain laws.

This portrait of Taft and his family was made shortly after he won the 1908 election. From left to right are Helen, Charlie, Mrs. Nellie Taft, Robert Taft, and the president.

Because he liked to consider issues so carefully, Taft also tended to procrastinate, or wait until it was too late to act. This angered some of the progressives, who felt Taft was not working hard enough to promote their programs. It looked as if Taft's presidency would be a difficult one.

WILLIAM TAFT WAS THE largest president in American history. The Tafts installed a specially designed bathtub in the White House for him. It was large enough to fit three grown men. They also installed an oversized bathtub in his home in the Philippines. Despite his size, Taft remained agile and athletic. He was considered a good dancer, and he played tennis and golf.

Taft's weight problem was caused by stress. He overate during difficult times and then slimmed down when he was happy. He was at his heaviest close to the end of his presidency. Later, as a professor and Supreme Court justice, he lost weight.

As with other tough problems in his life, Taft tried to keep a sense of humor about his size. While in the Philippines, he sent a message to Secretary of War Elihu Root about his travels. He reported that the trip had gone well, even though he had ridden on horseback high into the mountains for 25 miles. Root sent a message back asking, "How is the horse?" Taft thought the remark was humorous, and he even passed on the story to newspaper reporters.

Chapter FOUR

Failure and Success

Shortly after Taft was inaugurated, he suffered a personal setback. Mrs. Taft collapsed. Afterward, she temporarily lost the ability to talk. Nellie's illness devastated Taft, who had relied on her strength and judgment so often in the past.

TAFT IS NOT KNOWN AS A SUCCESSFUL PRESIDENT, but he actually accomplished a great deal. Two states, New Mexico and Arizona, were admitted into the **union** during his presidency. He helped pass laws to make working conditions safer for railroad and mine workers. He wanted to reduce the workday to eight hours for government employees. Taft was also the first president to appoint a woman to head a **bureau** in the **federal** government. He appointed Julia Lathrop to head the children's bureau of the Labor Department.

President Taft tried to expand U.S. business interests into other parts of the world. He encouraged bankers and businessmen to invest in foreign countries. This became known as "dollar **diplomacy**" because Taft

Taft won the nation's most important political office in only the second election of his life. "If I were now presiding in the Supreme Court," said Taft, "I would feel entirely at home." The presidency was a different matter. "I feel just a little bit like a fish out of water," he joked.

President Taft and Vice President James Sherman attended a baseball game together in 1909. Unfortunately, Taft had few such pleasant days during his term of office. His presidency was difficult, and he was unhappy.

hoped to use money instead of warfare to make the country more powerful overseas.

Taft continued Roosevelt's efforts to break up **trusts.** Trusts allowed businesses to grow so huge that they could control the **market.** Some trusts were monopolies, or large companies with so much power that smaller companies could not compete. Monopolies often put other companies out of business.

Although he had some success, Taft also had many problems. He was a poor politician who had trouble making Congress agree with his ideas. An example was his effort to pass a tariff bill. Tariffs are taxes on goods that are **imported** from other countries. Taft asked Congress to pass a bill that would lower these taxes. U.S. businesses liked high tariffs because it meant more people would buy their goods. But the progressives wanted lower tariffs so more Americans could afford imported goods.

The progressives tried hard to pass the bill to lower tariffs. The conservatives tried just as hard to stop it from passing. Although Taft worked to improve the bill, he did not try to convince Congress to pass it.

Congress debated the issue for months. Finally, it passed the Payne-Aldrich tariff bill. This bill was a **compromise.** Neither the conservatives nor the progressives really got what they wanted. The bill cut tariffs on most items but raised tariffs on others.

The Tafts were the last presidential family to keep a dairy cow at the White House. "Pauline," as she was called, often grazed on the White House lawn.

This photograph shows the White House in 1909. Taft was the first president to move his office from the main White House into the newly built West Wing. During his term, he also had the Oval Office constructed.

Taft knew the bill was not exactly what his party wanted, but he thought it improved the situation overall. The newspapers did not see it that way. They attacked Taft as a **traitor** to his party. Still, Taft did not defend himself or the bill.

Taft ran into another sticky problem dealing with land **conservation.** At that time, there were still many thousands of acres of wild land in the United States. People could homestead, claiming land as theirs simply by settling on it. The government could keep land if it had natural **resources,** such as minerals or oil. President Roosevelt had set aside large amounts of land. Some of this land did not have resources. The head of the U.S. Forest Service, Gifford Pinchot, was pleased that the former president had secured land for national forests and parks.

When Taft became president, his **secretary of the interior,** Richard A. Ballinger, was careful about what land he claimed for the government. He only set aside lands that were proven to have valuable resources. This angered Pinchot. It also upset a man named Louis R. Glavis, who worked with Ballinger at the Department of the Interior. Both men wanted to keep more land for the government, especially for parks and forests.

Glavis accused Ballinger of helping oil companies take land away from the government. Taft stepped in to solve the argument. In his judge-like manner, he looked at evidence and listened to both sides. In the end, both Taft and the U.S. Congress found that Ballinger had done nothing wrong. In fact, Glavis had been dishonest. He had hidden information that could prove Ballinger was innocent of the charges. Ballinger fired Glavis, and Taft approved of the decision.

Glavis was angry and spoke to reporters, who ran the story without checking to see if the facts were correct. Pinchot continued to support Glavis. At this point, Taft had no choice but to fire Pinchot. Unfortunately, Roosevelt had appointed him. Firing him made Taft look as if he were turning against the progressives and against Roosevelt. In addition, Taft had appointed many new cabinet members after his election, letting go many of Roosevelt's trusted advisors.

Taft began to lose the support of many progressive Republicans. Without them, he had to turn to the conservative Republicans for advice and help. This angered the progressives even more.

In 1910, Theodore Roosevelt returned from a lengthy African safari. He discovered that the Republican Party was a mess. He made negative statements about how Taft was performing as president. This wounded Taft. "I am deeply hurt," he said. "And it is hard, very hard … to see a devoted friendship going to pieces."

By the next presidential election in 1912, Taft had lost Roosevelt's backing. He and Roosevelt were no longer friends. The stress from these problems caused Taft to overeat. Near the end of his term as president, Taft's weight ballooned to 355 pounds.

As president, Taft still had enough support to be nominated as the Republican Party candidate in 1912. Roosevelt started his own party to run against Taft. He called it the Progressive Party, also known as the Bull Moose Party. Splitting the Republican Party also split the votes. In the end, the Democratic candidate, Woodrow Wilson, easily won the election. Unfortunately, Roosevelt and Taft never renewed their friendship.

A political cartoon from Roosevelt's term of office depicted him as a king, holding Taft—the "prince" who would take over the "king's" throne. Roosevelt helped Taft during the campaign for the 1908 election. By 1910, Roosevelt said his support of Taft might have been a mistake.

Instead of being disappointed by his defeat, Taft was relieved. He was happy to leave politics. He became a professor at Yale University and he spent eight years teaching, writing books, and lecturing. He wrote a book about the presidency, called *Our Chief Magistrate and His Powers,* that is still a respected work.

In 1921, Taft fulfilled a lifelong dream when President Warren Harding appointed him chief justice of the United States Supreme Court. Taft is remembered as one of the most effective chief justices in U.S. history. He moved cases quickly through the court and worked tirelessly every day. He even convinced the government to pay for a beautiful new building for the Supreme Court.

Chief Justice Taft, extremely happy on the job, dropped a good deal of weight. He kept himself at a steady 244 pounds. He held the position of chief justice for more than eight years. Taft's success on the Supreme Court erased the unhappiness he felt as president. "I don't remember that I ever was president," he wrote shortly before his death.

For years, Taft had suffered from digestive problems and small heart attacks. He did not

want to retire, even though he was very ill. Taft finally left his position on the Supreme Court only a month before his death. He died on March 8, 1930, in Washington, D.C. He was 72 years old.

William Taft was buried at Arlington National Cemetery in Virginia. His wife Nellie lived for 13 years after her husband's death. She traveled and watched her children carry on the Taft tradition of education and the law. She died on May 22, 1943, at the age of 82.

Interesting Facts

▸ The home where William Howard Taft was born and raised in Cincinnati, Ohio, is now a National Historic Site. Many of the details about the home's decorations and furniture came from the many letters that the Taft family exchanged with one another.

1857 Taft is born to Alphonso and Louise Taft in Cincinnati, Ohio, on September 15. He is the couple's first child. Alphonso also has two sons from his first marriage.

1878 William Taft graduates from Yale University.

1879 Taft meets Helen "Nellie" Herron, the woman he will later marry.

1880 Taft graduates from Cincinnati Law School and becomes licensed to practice law.

1882 President Chester Arthur appoints Taft tax collector.

1886 Taft marries Helen "Nellie" Herron on June 19.

1887 Taft is appointed to the Ohio Superior Court.

1890 President Harrison appoints Taft U.S. solicitor general, an assistant to the nation's most important attorney, the attorney general.

1892 Taft becomes a judge on the U.S. Sixth Circuit Court of Appeals. As a circuit court judge, he rules frequently on labor issues.

1900 Taft is appointed president of the U.S. Commission to establish order in the Philippines. He, his wife, and their three children travel to Manila, where they will live for the next four years.

1901 Taft becomes governor of the Philippines, appointed by President William McKinley. During his term, he helps construct roads, organize local governments, and set up schools, courts, and basic services for the people. In September, President McKinley is assassinated. Theodore Roosevelt becomes the new president. He offers Taft a position on the Supreme Court, but Taft decides to stay in the Philippines.

1904 President Theodore Roosevelt appoints Taft to his cabinet as secretary of war. The two men become friends and confidants.

1908 Roosevelt encourages Taft to run for president. Although Taft is reluctant, he accepts the challenge. With Roosevelt's backing, Taft wins the Republican Party's nomination for president. During his campaign, he promises tariff reform if he becomes president.

1909 Taft is inaugurated the 27th president of the United States. He urges Congress to reduce tariffs, and a battle among progressives and conservatives begins. A compromise, the Payne-Aldrich Tariff, is finally signed into law, but it does not give either the conservatives or the progressives what they really want.

1910 Roosevelt returns from an extended trip in Africa and finds the Republican Party in trouble. He is angered to learn that President Taft fired a man he had appointed during his own presidency, head of the U.S. Forest Service Gifford Pinchot. Taft and Roosevelt begin to have differences of opinion.

1912 Taft establishes the children's bureau of the Department of Labor. He appoints Julia Lathrop its head. She is the first woman to head a department bureau. New Mexico and Arizona are admitted to the union. Roosevelt starts his own political party to run against Taft for the presidency. Both Taft and Roosevelt lose the election to Democrat Woodrow Wilson. Taft receives fewer votes than any other sitting president in history.

1913 Taft accepts a position as professor of constitutional law at Yale University. He will hold the position for the next eight years.

1921 Taft is appointed chief justice of the U.S. Supreme Court by President Warren Harding.

1930 Taft retires from the Supreme Court on February 3. On March 8th, he dies at age 72.

1943 On May 22, Helen "Nellie" Herron Taft dies at age 82.

apply (uh-PLY)
If people apply for a job, they ask for it. Taft only applied for one job during his life.

appointed (uh-POIN-ted)
If someone is appointed to a position, he or she is asked by an important official to accept the position. President Harding appointed Taft as the chief justice of the Supreme Court.

assassinate (uh-SASS-uh-nayt)
To assassinate means to murder someone, especially a well-known person. Taft was upset when he learned that President McKinley had been assassinated.

bills (BILZ)
Bills are ideas for new laws that are presented to a group of lawmakers. Congress and the president decide if bills will become laws.

bureau (BYUR-oh)
A bureau is a division within a government department. Taft appointed Julia Lathrop to head the children's bureau of the Labor Department.

cabinet (KAB-eh-net)
A cabinet is the group of people who advise a president. As the secretary of war, Taft was a member of President Roosevelt's cabinet.

campaign (kam-PAYN)
A campaign is the process of running for an election, including activities such as giving speeches or attending rallies. Taft said a presidential campaign was a nightmare.

candidate (KAN-deh-det)
A candidate is a person who is running in an election. Several candidates run for president every four years.

chief executive (CHEEF eg-ZEK-yuh-tiv)
The chief executive is another name for the president. The president heads the executive branch of the U.S. government, which decides which laws are put into effect.

chief justice (CHEEF JUS-tiss)
The chief justice is the leader of a court. Taft served as chief justice of the U.S. Supreme Court.

circuit court (SUR-kit KORT)
A circuit court is one that sends judges to different locations to hear trials. Taft was appointed to the U.S. Circuit Court, which meant that he had to travel to different cities.

commission (kuh-MISH-un)
A commission is a group of people appointed to do something. Taft served as president of the commission sent to help the Filipino people.

compromise (KOM-pruh-myz)
If people compromise, they settle a difference of opinion by agreeing that both sides will give up part of what they want. The Payne-Aldrich bill was a compromise because neither side got exactly what it wanted.

conservation (kon-ser-VAY-shun)
Conservation is the practice of protecting something from being lost or used up. The progressive Republicans believed in land conservation.

conservative (kun-SER-vuh-tiv)
In politics, a conservative is someone who wants to make few changes in the government. President Taft began to meet with the conservative Republicans when he lost support from the progressive Republicans.

diplomacy (dih-PLOH-muh-see)
Diplomacy is when a government uses careful actions to make sure it gets along with other nations. Taft used "dollar diplomacy" to improve relations with other countries.

federal (FED-ur-ul)
Federal means having to do with the central government of the United States, rather than a state or city government. Taft was the first president to elect a woman to an important federal government position.

imported (im-POR-ted)
If a product is imported, it has been brought in from a foreign country for sale or use. Tariffs on imported goods made them more expensive to buy than American goods.

inauguration (ih-naw-gyuh-RAY-shun)
An inauguration is the ceremony that takes place when a new president begins a term of office. The weather was bad on Taft's inauguration day.

labor unions (LAY-bor YOON-yenz)
Labor unions are groups of workers who join together to try to improve working conditions. Labor unions and businesses often disagreed during the late 1800s.

market (MAR-kit)
A market is the buying and selling of a specific product. Some companies controlled a market for a certain product by owning many smaller businesses that made the same product.

nomination (nom-ih-NAY-shun)
If someone receives a nomination, he or she is chosen by a political party to run for an office. Taft won the presidential nomination of the Republican Party in 1908.

**political party
(puh-LIT-uh-kul PAR-tee)**
A political party is a group of people who share similar ideas about how to run a government. Today, as in Taft's time, the two major U.S. political parties are the Democrats and the Republicans.

politics (PAWL-uh-tiks)
Politics refers to the actions and practices of the government. Taft preferred to work in law rather than in politics.

progressive (pruh-GRESS-iv)
A progressive is a person who believes in making changes in government. Taft and Roosevelt believed in progressive ideas.

prosecutor (PRAH-seh-kyoo-tur)
A prosecutor is a lawyer who works for the government. Taft was appointed assistant prosecutor of Hamilton County.

radical (RAD-uh-kul)
If an idea is radical, it is very different from the way things are usually done. William Jennings Bryan had radical ideas about government.

resources (REE-sor-sez)
Resources are things that can be used to benefit people, such as oil or water. The government often controls land with valuable natural resources.

revolution (rev-uh-LOO-shun)
A revolution is something that causes a complete change in government. Rebels led a revolution in Cuba.

rule (ROOL)
If a judge rules on something, he or she makes a decision during a trial. Taft ruled on many labor issues as a circuit court judge.

secretary of the interior (SEK-ruh-tair-ee OF THE in-TEER-ee-ur)
The secretary of the interior is a member of the president's cabinet. He or she heads the department in charge of how U.S. land is used.

secretary of war (SEK-ruh-tair-ee OF WAR)
The secretary of war was once a member of the president's cabinet. This person helped the president make decisions about how to defend the country. Today the secretary of war is known as the secretary of defense.

solicitor (suh-LIS-uh-tur)
A solicitor is another word for a lawyer. President Harrison named Taft the solicitor general.

strike (STRYK)
If workers strike, they refuse to do their jobs until their employers agree to something. Workers might strike for better pay or shorter hours, for example.

Supreme Court (suh-PREEM KORT)
The Supreme Court is the highest court in the United States, which means it is more powerful than all other American courts. There are nine justices (judges) on the Supreme Court.

traitor (TRAY-ter)
A traitor is a person who betrays his or her country. Some people said Taft was a traitor to his party.

treaty (TREE-tee)
A treaty is a formal agreement that is made between nations. In the treaty that ended the Spanish-American War, Spain gave the United States control of the Philippine Islands.

trusts (TRUSTS)
Trusts are two or more companies that make an agreement to work together. Generally, trusts attempt to put other companies out of business to get more business for themselves.

union (YOON-yen)
A union is the joining together of two or more people or groups of people, such as states. The United States is also known as the Union.

Our PRESIDENTS

President	Birthplace	Life Span	Presidency	Political Party	First Lady
George Washington	Virginia	1732–1799	1789–1797	None	Martha Dandridge Custis Washington
John Adams	Massachusetts	1735–1826	1797–1801	Federalist	Abigail Smith Adams
Thomas Jefferson	Virginia	1743–1826	1801–1809	Democratic-Republican	widower
James Madison	Virginia	1751–1836	1809–1817	Democratic Republican	Dolley Payne Todd Madison
James Monroe	Virginia	1758–1831	1817–1825	Democratic Republican	Elizabeth Kortright Monroe
John Quincy Adams	Massachusetts	1767–1848	1825–1829	Democratic-Republican	Louisa Johnson Adams
Andrew Jackson	South Carolina	1767–1845	1829–1837	Democrat	widower
Martin Van Buren	New York	1782–1862	1837–1841	Democrat	widower
William H. Harrison	Virginia	1773–1841	1841	Whig	Anna Symmes Harrison
John Tyler	Virginia	1790–1862	1841–1845	Whig	Letitia Christian Tyler Julia Gardiner Tyler
James K. Polk	North Carolina	1795–1849	1845–1849	Democrat	Sarah Childress Polk

Our PRESIDENTS

President	Birthplace	Life Span	Presidency	Political Party	First Lady
Zachary Taylor	Virginia	1784–1850	1849–1850	Whig	Margaret Mackall Smith Taylor
Millard Fillmore	New York	1800–1874	1850–1853	Whig	Abigail Powers Fillmore
Franklin Pierce	New Hampshire	1804–1869	1853–1857	Democrat	Jane Means Appleton Pierce
James Buchanan	Pennsylvania	1791–1868	1857–1861	Democrat	never married
Abraham Lincoln	Kentucky	1809–1865	1861–1865	Republican	Mary Todd Lincoln
Andrew Johnson	North Carolina	1808–1875	1865–1869	Democrat	Eliza McCardle Johnson
Ulysses S. Grant	Ohio	1822–1885	1869–1877	Republican	Julia Dent Grant
Rutherford B. Hayes	Ohio	1822–1893	1877–1881	Republican	Lucy Webb Hayes
James A. Garfield	Ohio	1831–1881	1881	Republican	Lucretia Rudolph Garfield
Chester A. Arthur	Vermont	1829–1886	1881–1885	Republican	widower
Grover Cleveland	New Jersey	1837–1908	1885–1889	Democrat	Frances Folsom Cleveland

Our PRESIDENTS

President	Birthplace	Life Span	Presidency	Political Party	First Lady
Benjamin Harrison	Ohio	1833–1901	1889–1893	Republican	Caroline Scott Harrison
Grover Cleveland	New Jersey	1837–1908	1893–1897	Democrat	Frances Folsom Cleveland
William McKinley	Ohio	1843–1901	1897–1901	Republican	Ida Saxton McKinley
Theodore Roosevelt	New York	1858–1919	1901–1909	Republican	Edith Kermit Carow Roosevelt
William H. Taft	Ohio	1857–1930	1909–1913	Republican	Helen Herron Taft
Woodrow Wilson	Virginia	1856–1924	1913–1921	Democrat	Ellen L. Axson Wilson Edith Bolling Galt Wilson
Warren G. Harding	Ohio	1865–1923	1921–1923	Republican	Florence Kling De Wolfe Harding
Calvin Coolidge	Vermont	1872–1933	1923–1929	Republican	Grace Goodhue Coolidge
Herbert C. Hoover	Iowa	1874–1964	1929–1933	Republican	Lou Henry Hoover
Franklin D. Roosevelt	New York	1882–1945	1933–1945	Democrat	Anna Eleanor Roosevelt Roosevelt
Harry S. Truman	Missouri	1884–1972	1945–1953	Democrat	Elizabeth Wallace Truman

Our PRESIDENTS

President	Birthplace	Life Span	Presidency	Political Party	First Lady
Dwight D. Eisenhower	Texas	1890–1969	1953–1961	Republican	Mary "Mamie" Doud Eisenhower
John F. Kennedy	Massachusetts	1917–1963	1961–1963	Democrat	Jacqueline Bouvier Kennedy
Lyndon B. Johnson	Texas	1908–1973	1963–1969	Democrat	Claudia Alta Taylor Johnson
Richard M. Nixon	California	1913–1994	1969–1974	Republican	Thelma Catherine Ryan Nixon
Gerald Ford	Nebraska	1913–	1974–1977	Republican	Elizabeth "Betty" Bloomer Warren Ford
James Carter	Georgia	1924–	1977–1981	Democrat	Rosalynn Smith Carter
Ronald Reagan	Illinois	1911–	1981–1989	Republican	Nancy Davis Reagan
George Bush	Massachusetts	1924–	1989–1993	Republican	Barbara Pierce Bush
William Clinton	Arkansas	1946–	1993–2001	Democrat	Hillary Rodham Clinton
George W. Bush	Connecticut	1946–	2001–	Republican	Laura Welch Bush

Presidential FACTS

Qualifications

To run for president, a candidate must
- be at least 35 years old
- be a citizen who was born in the United States
- have lived in the United States for 14 years

Term of Office

A president's term of office is four years. No president can stay in office for more than two terms.

Election Date

The presidential election takes place every four years on the first Tuesday of November.

Inauguration Date

Presidents are inaugurated on January 20.

Oath of Office

I do solemnly swear I will faithfully execute the office of the President of the United States and will to the best of my ability preserve, protect, and defend the Constitution of the United States.

Write a Letter to the President

One of the best things about being a U.S. citizen is that Americans get to participate in their government. They can speak out if they feel government leaders aren't doing their jobs. They can also praise leaders who are going the extra mile. Do you have something you'd like the president to do? Should the president worry more about the environment and encourage people to recycle? Should the government spend more money on our schools? You can write a letter to the president to say how you feel!

1600 Pennsylvania Avenue
Washington, D.C. 20500

You can even send an e-mail to: president@whitehouse.gov

For Further INFORMATION

Internet Sites

Learn more about Taft as president and read his inaugural address:
http://www.bartleby.com/sv/welcom.html

Read Taft's messages to Congress and learn more about his Supreme Court decisions:
http://www.interlink-café.com/uspresident/27th.htm

Visit the Taft's Summer White House in Beverly, Massachusetts:
http://www.members.tripod.com/BevHistSoc/

Find out how to visit the house where Taft was born and raised, now called the William Howard Taft Historic Site:
http://www.nps.gov/wiho/

Learn more about all the Supreme Court Justices:
http://supct.law.cornell.edu:8080/supct/cases/judges.htm

Learn more about all the presidents and visit the White House:
http://www.whitehouse.gov/WH/glimpse/presidents/html/presidents.html
http://www.thepresidency.org/presinfo.htm
http://www.americanpresidents.org

Books

Bachrach, Deborah. *The Spanish-American War.* San Diego, CA: Lucent Books, 1991.

Blue, Rose and Corinne J. Naden. *The White House Kids.* Brookfield, CT: Millbrook Press, 1995.

Brittan, Dolly. *The People of the Philippines* (Celebrating the Peoples and Civilizations of Southeast Asia). New York: Power Kids Press, 1998.

Casey, Jane Clark. *William Howard Taft.* Danbury, CT: Childrens Press, 1989.

Feinberg, Barbara Silberdick. *America's First Ladies.* Danbury, CT: Franklin Watts, 1998.

Feinburg, Barbara Silberdick. *The Cabinet.* New York: Twenty-First Century Books, 1995.

Stein, Conrad R. *Powers of the Supreme Court.* Danbury, CT: Childrens Press, 1995.

Index